SISTERS

Who

PRAY

**UNLEASHING THE POWER OF
FAITH THROUGH PRAYER**

DR. PAULETTE HARPER

THY WORD PUBLISHING

Published by Thy Word Publishing
Antioch, CA 94531

© 2025 Dr. Paulette Harper

Book Cover Design: Tyora Moody

Interior Book Design & Formatting:
https://tywebbincreations.com

Editor: Emile Kline
http://ekediting.com/

Literary Strategist: Dr. Paulette Harper Visit to access information about writing your own book.

SISTERS WHO PRAY

1973, 1978, 1984, 2011 by Biblica, Inc.TM. Used by permission of Zondervan

Library of Congress Cataloging-in-Publication Data

Paperback: ISBN: 979-8-218-62961-8

Published and printed in the United States of America.

CONTENTS

ACKNOWLEDGMENTS

With a heart full of gratitude, I extend my deepest appreciation to the incredible women of *Sisters Who Pray*. This journey would not be the same without each of you—your faith, your prayers, and your unwavering support have been a source of strength and inspiration.

To my prayer sisters, thank you for standing in the gap, interceding with boldness, and believing in the power of prayer. Your dedication to lifting others up in faith has been a testimony of God's love and grace.

To every woman who has poured her heart into this book, shared her testimony, and prayed fervently—your obedience to God's call is transforming lives. Your words will encourage, heal, and ignite the faith of many.

To my family, friends, and ministry partners—thank you for your prayers, love, and encouragement. Your support has carried me through this journey, and I am forever grateful.

Above all, I give thanks to God, who has orchestrated every connection, every prayer, and every word written on these pages. May this book serve as a beacon of hope, drawing women closer to Him.

With love and gratitude,

Dr. Paulette Harper, Visionary Author
www.pauletteharper.com

Visit to access a free resource to help you start writing your bestseller.

A Heartfelt Thank You to Our Sponsors

We are deeply grateful for the generous support of our sponsors. Your commitment to empowering women through faith, prayer, and community makes **Sisters Who Pray** possible. Your partnership ensures that we can continue to uplift and inspire others on their spiritual journey. Thank you for being a vital part of this transformative project.

Alicia Longmire

Adrian Clark

Arlena English

Aida Irizarry

Angela Madison

Anthonette Borges

Anthony Ramos

Anthony "Sonny" and Mey Ramos

Arlene Cajulao

Arlene Zamora

Bella Rose Ramos

Cynthia Little

Cathy Callender

Charlita Rivas

Cheryl Combs

Christina Aquilar

Christopher Ramos

Corazon Tabernero

Cristina Bulatao

Damonte Thomas

DeeVon Carmouche

Dwayne Kelly

Dan Nifalar

Daniel "DBoy" Nifalar

Daphne Risso

Donna Yates

Dorothy Jones

Dorothy Ross

Elisa Marty

Emily Calica

Eric and Corynna Tabernero

Faith Azalea Ramos

Geneva Gonzales

Gloria Gamulo

Julie Henry

Janneth Nicholas

Jannette Corpus

Jean Riley

Kathleen Slawson

Kornique Geter

Kiana Cruz

LaShon McGee

LaJoy Lindsey

Laura Dorsey

Laura Saga

Lilani Medalle

Lily Jazz Ramos

Linda Pajarillo

Margaret Kirk

Mariama Wurie

Mildred Bonds

Merian Marana Droesch

Noreen Constantino

Omar Hayes

Patrice Burrell

Patricia Hood

Patrick Nifalar

A Heartfelt Thank You to Our Sponsors

We are deeply grateful for the generous support of our sponsors. Your commitment to empowering women through faith, prayer, and community makes *Sisters Who Pray* possible. Your partnership ensures that we can continue to uplift and inspire others on their spiritual journey. Thank you for being a vital part of this transformative project.

Reginald Howard

Ron Henson

Roberta Cook

Rochie Gonzales

Roderick Von King

Rosita Caballero

Tina Lee

Valerie Clemmer

Virginia Agasa Asay

Zayin Tabernero

Z'Lijah Tabernero

Zoe Tabernero

A Message from the Visionary Author

Dr. Paulette Harper

Nineteen-Times Best-Selling Author | Speaker | Pastor | Literary Strategist

In a world filled with challenges and uncertainty, prayer becomes a powerful anchor, grounding us in faith and guiding us through life's storms with grace and strength. It is through prayer and unwavering belief that we find the courage to overcome obstacles, embrace our purpose, and walk boldly in God's divine plan.

Within the pages of *Sisters Who Pray*, we celebrate the remarkable testimonies of women who have experienced the transformative power of prayer. Through faith-filled perseverance, they have navigated trials, conquered adversity, and witnessed the hand of God moving in their lives. These stories are a testament to the undeniable truth that when women pray, miracles happen, chains break, and lives are forever changed.

Our co-authors come from diverse walks of life, each bringing unique experiences that reflect the beauty of God's work in different seasons and circumstances. Their journeys remind us that prayer is not just a lifeline in difficult times—it is the key to unlocking breakthroughs, healing, and divine provision.

As you immerse yourself in these powerful stories, I invite you to reflect on your own journey of faith and the ways prayer has shaped your life. May these testimonies strengthen your belief, ignite your passion for intercession, and inspire you to stand boldly as a woman of prayer.

It is my honor to share these stories with you, with the hope that they encourage you to embrace a life filled with steadfast faith, unshakable courage, and the unwavering power of prayer.

Your Visionary Author,

Dr. Paulette Harper

Visit https://pauletteharper.com/signaturestoryworkbook/ to access a free recourse for aspiring authors.

When Prayer Calms the Storm

Dr. Paulette Harper

Can you recall a time when you were caught in a storm, where it felt like the tempest would never relent? Perhaps you know that feeling all too well, especially when trials seem to roll in one after the other, leaving you barely a moment to catch your breath. Among these tempests that life throws our way are some that permanently etch themselves into our memories. Out of all the storms I've weathered, one stands out distinctly above the rest.

Have you ever embarked on a journey of faith, acting upon what you believed to be a divine message, only to find yourself grappling with the urge to retreat halfway through? You want to slam on the brakes, shift into reverse, and begin anew. The path unfolding before you seems distant from your initial expectations. Every unraveling scene whispers that you might have misunderstood the signs. Apprehension takes root, and the doors of doubt and anxiety push open the chambers of your heart. Prior to taking that step of faith, your confidence in what you were doing was strong and unquenchable. Yet all along, God knew exactly what trouble awaited you. What problems were in the making. And He knew you would be in a place of doubt and disbelief. You began questioning whether God told you to do this. Did you really hear God? For sure? If God told you, then there shouldn't be any problems. No challenges, no regrets, right? On the contrary. In those places, be assured—God has us right where He wants us. In places of trouble. In that place where His still-quiet voice is not speaking.

This place will stretch your faith. God's promises will be challenged or questioned. In this place, going back seems like the better solution. At least, that's what your mind wants you to believe. Clearly, what's in front is more difficult than what's behind.

Storms and hindrances obscure our view, tainting our vision so retreating feels safer. Retreating feels more comfortable. Retreating appears more in reach. Have you been there?

Years ago, I relocated back to California. I thought those closest to me would be excited about my return. Don't get me wrong. At first, they were. But I soon learned I had entered a storm that would rock my world.

I moved in with people close to me. Mistake. Number. One. Suppressed bitterness and pent-up anger can contaminate a person's soul if not checked. The enemy speaks through people, bringing up old issues and reminding us of our pasts. I couldn't believe this was happening to me. I was blindsided. The words coming out of their mouths penetrated my heart and invoked fear when anger was aroused. Or worse, took it to a totally different level. When the enemy entices people, the situation can spin out of control.

I realized issues had been lying dormant. Years of unforgiveness. Years of covering over scars and years of bitterness that had spread like cancer. It was obvious something else was happening behind the scenes. Something fueled all this hostility, this opposition, and these outbursts.

The mind would have me believe the same people who once laughed with me, loved me, and ate with me were now my adversaries, my oppressors, my haters. But they were not.

"For we wrestle not against flesh and blood, but against principalities, against powers, against the rulers of the darkness of this world, against spiritual wickedness in high places" (Ephesians 6:12 KJV).

My focus and attention needed to extend beyond what my eyes saw and my ears heard. Although I wanted to use physical methods to fight, I knew these battles would not be won in the same fashion. I remained calm and reserved my emotional break outlet for the privacy of my prayer closet.

When I got saved, I had no idea I would endure such hostility, fight so many battles, and shed so many tears. I had been in many battles before, but this one pushed me to my physical, mental, and spiritual limits. One evening, I packed up a few things and left to stay with another relative. Once I got settled, I finally broke. I couldn't hold back the tears.

Those last few hours had taken an emotional toll on me. I had so many questions for God. I couldn't understand why He had allowed this to happen to me. What did I do to deserve this? What lessons was He teaching me? Some of life's lessons come from painful experiences. And in those experiences, I have come to know God is most concerned about my attitude, my response, and my behavior.

How would I respond when I saw them again? During the whole confrontation, He was there. He protected me from any physical harm. No, I didn't deserve that. But I couldn't allow what they did to stop me from doing what I needed to do. So, between the sobs, the hurt, and the pain, I prayed for them. I asked God to forgive them according to Matthew 5:44 KJV.

"But I say unto you, Love your enemies, bless them that curse you, do good to them that hate you, and pray for them which despitefully use you, and persecute you."

They thought they had the upper hand, and I'm sure they rejoiced at the confrontation. The entire episode perplexed me, and I had no idea what would come next, what crested the horizon, and what lurked behind the doors. Over the weekend, I scheduled my return to the home to pick up the rest of my belongings.

When I walked into the room, I found it occupied by someone else. Right then and there was my "aha" moment when all the pieces came together. The moment I looked face-to-face at another person I had nurtured. My heart dropped. I was speechless. I was numb. I stood in the doorway in total disbelief. I just couldn't believe it was getting worse. I felt betrayed. I had been duped, deceived, and tricked by someone I loved. Had I been set up? Why had I not seen this coming? The fight had just intensified. Now, I had to add someone else to my prayer list. Was I emotionally ready to face this? To tell you the truth, this had nothing to do with my emotions or feelings. It was all spiritual warfare. All the teachings, the sermons, and the notetaking were now being tested.

I've been saved long enough and have walked through enough hard situations to know the greater the struggle and the challenges, the greater the blessings. The enemy would not fight me as hard, use those close to me, and put roadblocks in my way if God's blessings were not great. In the midst of receiving blessings in life, we sometimes encounter the worst in life.

Amid it all, we might find ourselves tempted to succumb to bitterness and hatred, to let go of prayer and embrace despair, hopelessness, and anguish. But let me tell you, God expects us to pray—no ifs, ands, or buts about it. My unbreakable spirit refused to let these battles and storms push me into despair or rob me of hope. It doesn't matter who the devil employs, what fiery arrows he hurls, or what cunning schemes he devises.

I'm here to declare that victory is mine—and yours, too.

Past victories weren't won easily or by waving a white flag. They were earned by standing strong against every opposition and applying the lessons learned from the Word of God. I refused to be swayed away from God's promises by these storms. They wouldn't push me to abandon my faith. In fact, this storm taught me to place my trust in God and pray without ceasing. The result? Blessings beyond measure, starting with a renewed sense of purpose, a deeper connection with God, and clarity about His plans for my life.

This journey showed me that prayer isn't just about asking for help—it's about strengthening your relationship with God. It's about leaning on Him fully when the world around you crumbles. And most importantly, it's about standing firm in your faith, knowing that God's promises never fail. If you're facing your own storm, remember that prayer is your anchor. It is the lifeline that will keep you steady when the waves threaten to overtake you.

Takeaways from this story:

1. **Never underestimate the power of prayer**: It is not just a ritual; it's a source of strength and connection with God.

2. **Forgiveness is essential**: Holding on to bitterness only deepens your wounds. Let God's grace guide you to forgive others, even when it feels impossible.

3. **Recognize spiritual warfare**: Understand that your battles are not merely physical or emotional—they are spiritual. Equip yourself with God's Word and prayer to stand firm.

4. **Trust God's process**: Even when the road is tough and the outcome un-

clear, know that God is shaping you for something greater.

5. **Celebrate the victories**: No matter how small, every step forward is a testament to God's faithfulness. Hold on to those moments as reminders of His goodness.

About the Author

Dr. Paulette Harper is an ordained pastor in the Gospel, a nineteen-time best-selling, two-time award-winning author, and the founder of Faith Business Success Virtual Summits, whose mission is to provide speakers with exposure and visibility to share their message on a global platform. She is also a recipient of the 2024 RiseHer Presidential Lifetime Achievement Award and The Passion Purpose Peace Award presented by Her Excellency Dr. Theresa A. Mobley.

As the founder and CEO of Harper Media and Coaching Academy she serves as the self-publishing coach to nonfiction aspiring authors. She specializes in coaching women how to build their brand, expand their influence and publish a subject matter book that positions them as experts in their field.

Connect with Dr. Paulette Harper

- Website www.pauletteharper.com

- IG: https://www.instagram.com/dr.harperpaulette

- LinkedIn: https://www.linkedin.com/in/paulette-harper/

When Adversity Gave Birth to the Power of Prayer

Lakeea Kelly

I wanted a husband. God answered my prayers for others, and now it was my turn. Every day, I prayed for God to send me a husband. I even made a list, not just of the characteristics I wanted him to have, but down to what he would like and dislike. Can you believe I included he would love broccoli? I was always cooking broccoli, so of course he had to love it, too. He also needed to like sports, make me laugh, and, of course, be handsome—all these external desires, and somewhere on that list, he had to be a God-fearing man that loved my sons like his own. I trusted God to answer this prayer as He had answered all my prayers prior.

One evening, I was attending Bible study and saw a man I had never seen before. He was attractive, but I didn't have any thoughts beyond that. After Bible study, he approached me and asked for my phone number. I graciously gave it to him. I was single and hadn't dated in a very long time. At this point in my walk with the Lord, I was sold out for Jesus and celibate! We began conversing over the phone and spending a lot of quality time together. One day, he received a phone call when he was at my house. He excused himself to take the call and told me, "I need to pray for the individual that called me."

When I tell you, this man prayed—he prayed with such boldness, confidence, and power. He prayed like me. My attraction elevated. There was no doubt he would be my husband. I didn't need to confirm any other fruit in his life because I heard this man pray. Our conversations grew more intimate. Marriage was now the conversation.

One sunny day, within a couple of months or so of us dating, we were in the car headed to the store, and he asked me to marry him. There was nothing romantic about it, nothing memorable, and it certainly didn't seem thought out. I never imagined my proposal to be so unthoughtful. But, hey, I wasn't going to complain because I had prayed for a husband for so long. I had known him less than a year, and in five months, we were married.

Many family and friends didn't agree with this marriage; they felt something was off about this man. I didn't heed the warnings.

"It's just the devil using them to stop me from receiving my blessing." Have you ever ignored wise counsel from a trusted family member, friend, or leader because it wasn't what you wanted to hear? These people had my best interest at heart, but I didn't take the time to fast and pray about what so many people stated about my soon-to-be husband.

We got married in a storage building that was renovated for event, though I had always imagined a wedding on the beach. At least a wedding with all my family and friends present. Some family and friends attend, but nothing like I had imagined. Our first dance was so dry. The frosting on our cake melted, and the strawberries slid off the cake before we could cut it and serve the guests—we ended up throwing it away. During our honeymoon, he watched sports practically the entire time. (Remember how I wanted someone that loved sports? That was an understatement). It was a nice room with a jacuzzi, but he was watching sports. This was not the wedding of my dreams; this was not the desires of my heart.

Our so-called honeymoon was over before it began. The official storm commenced. The mask came off, revealing the true motives of his heart. This man, who was considered a minister of the gospel and a prayer warrior, became emotionally and mentally abusive toward me. Even the words he spoke over himself were demonic. He would often say, "I want a black heart." I had *never* heard someone say those words. It was pure demonic witchcraft! He destroyed things in our home and became jealous of my relationship with God. He threw my Bible on several occasions while yelling, "Go be with your God." It was as if he was angry with God and angry with me for serving the God he was angry with. He even raised his fists at me while yelling at the top of his lungs on several occassions, but my angels always protected me from physical abuse.

Despite the abuse, I stayed in prayer. I cried out to God in desperation many nights to release me from such misery. I repented over and over again, asking God to forgive me if I had married this man out of disobedience. I just wanted out. I didn't know how God would do it, but I trusted that he would.

At one point, we took a road trip to Nashville, TN, to see family. Out of jealousy, he argued about me spending time with family—one of the reasons we went. The day before we were scheduled to leave Nashville, I woke up and he was gone with my car. He had left me and my sons stranded in Nashville. Impacting my sons and making us feel unprotected was a huge red flag for. At that moment, I knew it was time to separate.

During our separation, which was not a legal separation, he cheated on me with a lady who attended our church. He didn't even try to be discrete about it. My sons saw him out in the public holding hands with this woman.

I felt so much shame and embarrassment. Remember in the beginning, when I said he checked off everything on my list? He checked off everything except for being a God-fearing man who walked in godly conduct and the fruit of the Spirit. Where was the fruit?

He checked off all the superficial qualities because those were the virtues in my heart. I set those things before spiritual things, I set those things before seeking the will of God, blinding myself to what truly sustains a relationship. Have you ever wanted a husband so badly that you ignored red flags, dismissed wise counsel, and neglected to seek Jesus Christ through prayer? Did the idol in your heart cloud your vision, keeping you from seeing God's best for you? What qualities are on *your* "list" for a spouse? Are they based on God's desire for you or your own?

I got myself in a mess due to the idols of my heart, and now I had to seek God in my affliction to release me from what was killing me spiritually and emotionally. I thought prayer was about asking God for whatever *I* wanted, and He would grant *my* desires according to *my* will, and not His, but that was the wrong interpretation of prayer. Prayer is a form of worship that draws us closer to God and grants us access to His Presence. Prayer is petitioning God according to His will, and it aligns us with God's heart.

My prayer was answered according to the idols in my heart. I never once asked for God's wisdom regarding my list. How *did* he feel about my list? How did he feel about the man I married? I dismissed the wise counsel God sent my way regarding this man and never took their words to God in prayer. I had finally got my husband, and nothing could change that.

Asking God for a husband wasn't a wrong desire, but my desire wasn't led by wisdom. A life of prayer that does not go beyond requesting external possessions is a prayer life that is rooted in idols of the heart. I sought *things*, not His Kingdom and righteousness first. "Seek the Kingdom of God above all else, and live righteously, and he will give you everything you need" (Matthew 6:33 NLT).

God teaches us what truly matters during afflictions and life's storms. During this unfortunate situation, I cried out to God, desperate for His help. I humbled myself in repentance, whether I believed I was wrong or not. Prayer is about humbling ourselves and allowing Him to show us our hidden sins that conflict with His will. This situation taught me to depend on God for what I need and not necessarily what I want because what I want is not always good for me. The desire to marry never left, but I settled in my spirit, waiting on God to give me who He knew was best for my life. The long list of requests changed to *God, give me what I need.*

I now have a true God-fearing husband who loves me and my sons like his own. He has the fruit of the Spirit and a good reputation in the city gates. He is a man full of wisdom, a protector, and a provider. Oh, and he makes me laugh, which is an awesome bonus. We had two weddings: a church wedding and a destination honeymoon where we recited our own vows on the beach. God exceeded my expectations; that is exactly what God does when we seek His will in prayer over our own. He will give you what you didn't ask for! God gave me just what I needed when I surrendered my will for His will through prayer.

Before entering any relationship, seek God's wisdom and ask Him to align your heart with His will. Prioritize spiritual compatibility over superficial qualities, remembering that God calls us to be equally yoked. "Do not be unequally yoked together with unbelievers. For what fellowship has righteousness with lawlessness? And what communion has light with darkness?" (2 Corinthians 6:14 NKJV). Reflect on whether your desires, expectations, or personal lists overshadow God's plans. Identify and release any idols through repentance that might be guiding your decisions. Understand that prayer is not a wish list but a way to align yourself with God's heart. Seek His guidance, and trust Him to provide what you *need*, and not just what you want.

About the Author

Lakeea Kelly is the CEO and founder of TransHERmation Academy, LLC, an assistant pastor, serving alongside her husband, Dwyane Kelly, at New Harvest Christian Center in Battle Creek, MI, author, Christian speaker, and life coach dedicated to helping women transform from the inside out through biblical principles.

With over twenty-two years of experience in the federal government, Lakeea holds a bachelor's degree in family life education, a master's degree in psychology with an emphasis in life coaching, and certifications in biblical counseling and life coaching.

As a global coach, she has empowered women worldwide to overcome challenges, discover their worth, and walk in their God-given purpose. She is the author of three transformational books, including *TransHERmation: How God Can Take Everything You've Been Through* and *Transform You for His Glory*.

Lakeea's message focuses on character development and biblical alignment. Having overcome rejection and depression, she equips women with practical keys to turn pain into triumph. Her unwavering commitment to helping women struggling with rejection and a lack of confidence makes her a guiding light in both her church and community.

Connect with Lakeea Kelly

- Website: www.lakeeakelly.com

- YouTube: http://www.youtube.com/ @lakeeakelly

- Facebook: facebook.com/Transhermation

THE REDEMPTION THAT FOUND ME THROUGH PRAYER

ATAVIA BARNES

Trauma, resilience, and the undeniable power of prayer mark my journey. For years, I endured verbal, emotional, mental, and physical abuse in a relationship that looked like love but was anything but. That toxic cycle nearly broke me, mirroring the destructive path of my biological mother, who had battled her own demons with addiction. Yet,

God was there through it all, and prayer became my lifeline to healing and deliverance.

I met the man I thought was my future through a cousin. At first glance, he seemed kind, gentle, and attentive; everything I believed love should be. For the first year, our relationship flourished. We attended church together, spent all our spare time with one another, and eventually moved in together. It felt like the perfect beginning. But then, his true nature began surfacing.

The abuse started subtly, with verbal insults that chipped away at my self-esteem. Over time, it escalated to shoves and pushes, and soon after, the violence heightened. He imposed strict rules on me, demanding that I meet his time frames and threatening me with violence if I didn't comply. Each time he hurt me, he would apologize, professing his love and blaming me for his actions. He convinced me that if I just obeyed him and didn't upset him, the abuse would stop.

This manipulation took a toll on me. His words tore me down until I believed that I was the problem, that I deserved the pain I endured. I hid the bruises and lied to protect him, defending his actions even as they destroyed me. The abuse wasn't just physical; it was mental and emotional, leaving scars that no one could see.

The darkest moment came when I was pregnant with his child. One night, in a fit of rage, he beat me until I lost consciousness and used a clothes hanger to terminate my pregnancy. My living son was already six years old when I conceived the child that was lost.

The grief and trauma from that loss were indescribable, yet I remained in the relationship. He continued harming me, stabbing me with a screwdriver, cutting me with a box cutter, and even pulling out my hair. Threats, apologies, and promises accompanied each act of violence, creating a cycle I couldn't seem to escape. He tried to force me into marriage, threatening to kill me and my son if I refused.

Out of fear, I unwillingly made plans to marry him. But God intervened. The night before the wedding, a family member caught him with another woman. That revelation gave me the courage to call off the wedding and walk away. It was my path to freedom, and I took it.

Though the physical abuse ended, the emotional and mental scars still haunted me. I had learned to mask my pain with a smile, pretending everything was fine when inside, I was broken. As I tried to rebuild my life, the enemy set another trap.

I met another young man who seemed promising. Our relationship lasted on and off for five years, but his struggles with drugs created a toxic dynamic. I wanted to help him, to believe that he could change, but the relationship became a soul tie that bound me for fourteen years. Each time he reappeared in my life, I let him back in, delaying my healing and growth.

The enemy knows what we desire and uses it to distract, deter, and delay God's plans for our lives. My relationships were distractions, pulling me away from God's purpose for me. I realized that connections are critical, and we must be discerning about who we allow into our lives.

One night, as I prepared to go to the club with my sister, my praying grandmother walked into the room. Her presence carried an unusual heaviness, and I could sense that something was different. She looked me in the eyes and said, "Cheri, the Lord told me to lift my prayers from you."

Her words hit me like a thunderclap, shaking me to my core. At first, I couldn't fully grasp the gravity of what she had said. Why would God instruct her to stop praying for me? But as I looked into her serious, unwavering eyes,

I realized she wasn't speaking lightly. This was a divine warning.

My heart sank, and a wave of conviction swept over me. I didn't argue or brush her off. Instead, I quietly turned back to my room, changed out of my club outfit, and put on my sleepwear. My sister, noticing my sudden change, asked why I wasn't going anymore. When I told her what our grandmother had said, she froze momentarily, then nodded. "If Grandma's not praying for us while we're in those streets, we don't need to go," she said. That was the last time I ever prepared to step foot in a club.

I didn't fully realize then that this was a pivotal turning point in my life. It was more than just a decision to stay home that night, it was the beginning of God calling me back to Himself. My grandmother's words pierced through the haze of distractions and bad decisions I had been living in, forcing me to reevaluate where I was headed. Her prayer life had been a covering for me, a shield that had likely kept me out of harm's way more times than I could count. But the thought of losing that covering left me exposed and vulnerable, and I didn't want to live outside of God's protection any longer.

Looking back on that night, I understand the power of my grandmother's prayers. The Bible says, "The prayer of a righteous person is powerful and effective" (James 5:16 NIV). Her prayers served as a lifeline, shielding me from the enemy's plans and leading me toward God's path of redemption. At the time, I didn't realize that God was already at work, providing a way out of a lifestyle that could have destroyed me. "No temptation has overtaken you except what is common to mankind. And God is faithful; he will not let you be tempted beyond what you can bear. But when you are tempted, he will also provide a way out so that you can endure it" (1 Corinthians 10:13 NIV). That night was my way out.

That night, I felt the weight of the life I was living. I realized how far I had strayed from God and how desperately I needed Him. It wasn't an instant transformation but the spark that ignited a deeper desire for change. Looking back, I know that moment wasn't just my grandmother's wisdom, it was God intervening once again, using her to offer me another chance to turn back to Him. Her obedience in delivering that message and my decision to listen altered my life's trajectory forever.

My grandmother became a crucial figure in my healing. She spoke to me about my future, and I realized I didn't have one. I had no dreams, no aspirations, just a broken past and an uncertain present. Her words challenged me to search my soul for better, and what I found was what I had left behind: God.

I wasn't sure if God would take me back after all I had done, but then I read the scripture, "I will never leave you nor forsake you" (Hebrews 13:5 NKJV). That promise gave me hope. Through prayer, I began rebuilding my relationship with Him. Prayer became my refuge, my source of strength, and the key to my deliverance.

As my grandmother and I had a heartfelt conversation about my life, she reminded me of God's promises and encouraged me to trust Him with my future. She reminded me of Proverbs 3:5-6 (NIV), which says, "Trust in the Lord with all your heart and lean not on your own understanding; in all your ways submit to him, and he will make your paths straight." For the first time, I realized I had been leaning on my own understanding, trying to navigate life without God. I didn't have dreams or aspirations because I had allowed the enemy to strip me of hope. But then I remembered Jeremiah 29:11 (NIV): "'For I know the plans I have for you,' declares the Lord, 'plans to prosper you and not to harm you, plans to give you hope and a future.'"

That verse planted a seed of hope in me—I began believing that God still had a plan for my life.

As I started to reflect and pray, I felt God drawing me closer to Him. "The righteous cry out, and the Lord hears them; he delivers them from all their troubles. The Lord is close to the brokenhearted and saves those who are crushed in spirit" (Psalm 34:17-18 NIV). I cried out to God, asking Him to forgive me and guide me back to where I belonged. Like the prodigal son, He welcomed me back with open arms. "But while he was still a long way off, his father saw him and was filled with compassion for him; he ran to his son, threw his arms around him and kissed him" (Luke 15:20 NIV). That was the love of God I experienced—a love that restored me, healed me, and gave me the courage to move forward.

God's grace carried me through the darkest moments of my life. He healed my wounds, restored my self-worth, and set me on a path of purpose. Today, I am free from the chains of abuse, toxic relationships, and self-doubt. I've learned that love doesn't hurt, and true love comes from God.

This journey has taught me the importance of prayer, the power of discernment, and the value of trusting God's plan. No matter how far we stray, His arms are always open, ready to welcome us home. Through Him, I found the strength to break free, heal, and live the life He always intended for me.

About the Author

Atavia Barnes is a multifaceted leader and trailblazer whose dynamic skill set spans entrepreneurship, professional excellence, and ministry. Recently elevated to chief administrative officer and overseer of Celebration of Praise Ministries, Inc., she demonstrates an unwavering commitment to excellence in every sphere of her influence.

As an entrepreneur, Atavia excels as a business consultant, executive administrator, road manager, conference strategist, and coach. Her gifts as a mentor, author, facilitator, editor, and content writer allow her to empower individuals and organizations to unlock their full potential.

In the professional realm, she has distinguished herself as a human resources and project manager, adept bookkeeper, and payroll administrator. Her ability to organize, manage, and execute complex operations has earned her a reputation for integrity and precision.

Atavia's ministry assignment as a prophet, Evangelist, and teacher reflects her deep passion for advancing God's Kingdom. She delivers prophetic insight, fosters spiritual growth, and equips others to fulfill their divine purpose.

Whether leading through her prophetic mantle, strategic vision, or professional expertise, Atavia Barnes remains steadfast in her mission to impact lives, build systems, and inspire change. She is a testament to servant leadership and Kingdom excellence.

Connect with Atavia

- Website: https://meetatavia.com

Pray...Trust...Wait— A Prayer Journey

Isabelle Ramos

As I journey through this life, prayer has become my survival kit, my oxygen, my source of strength and peace through every trial. In my brokenness, God meets me where I am. True prayer is not a ritual but a personal conversation with our Heavenly Father. He looks for honesty, for trust, for belief, and for faith. Through life's joys and sorrows, prayer became the foundation of my relationship with Jesus.

As a child, I was not brought up in a prayer-centered lifestyle. Religion taught me scripted prayers, words I had to memorize and recite. I thought prayer was repetition, duty, and obligation. I never realized that prayer was meant to be something deeper, something personal. I didn't understand that it was an invitation to a real, living relationship with God!

As I grew older and faced life's struggles—grief, family challenges, financial and health concerns—I began to seek more. The prayers I had memorized as a child didn't carry me through the pain I experienced. I needed more than just words; I needed connection. Prayer isn't about perfect words or religious formality. It's about pouring our hearts to the Lord, whether in joy, gratitude, anxiety, worry, concern, fear, or confusion.

In seasons of loss and uncertainty and through difficult decisions, I have learned to hold on to three powerful words: Pray. Trust. Wait.

During Covid, my heart shattered when my mother went home to be with the Lord. The pain of loss was heavy, and with the added burden of planning her funeral while my husband, Anthony, faced surgery, I felt stretched beyond my strength. My emotions overwhelmed me, and the weight of it all was more than I could bear on my own. I cried out to the Lord, and He met me in my grief, providing strength when I had none. In those moments of exhaustion, sorrow, and confusion, I turned to prayer, a conversation with God. Though the pain didn't disappear overnight, His presence gave me strength. As I leaned into Him, He carried me. Though grief still lingers, I know my mother is with my father, and they are both in God's presence, whole and at peace.

After my mother's celebration of life, Anthony's surgery was scheduled and successful. He was released within two days, though that same week, he was admitted back into the hospital, intubated, and kept in the ICU for nine days due to Covid. There were moments when I didn't know if Anthony would make it. Then I, too, contracted the virus. Fear and uncertainty surrounded me, but in my weakness, I turned to prayer. Surrendering my fears to the Lord was difficult, but in those darkest hours, I had to trust that God was in control. "Whenever I am afraid, I will trust in You" (Psalm 56:3 NKJV).

The waiting was painful; every moment felt like an eternity, but God reminded me He was at work, even in the silence. Even when I couldn't see the outcome, I trusted Him. He renewed my strength day by day, and in His perfect timing, He healed me and Anthony!

At the same time, I faced division in family relationships. Painful misunderstandings, broken connections, and the ache of seeing loved ones drift apart broke my heart. Knowing it was something I could not fix on my own, I prayed for reconciliation and restoration, for wisdom in my words, and for the ability to forgive, love, and seek peace even in the midst of hurt. Though the situation remains difficult, I am at peace knowing God is faithful even when I don't see immediate change. I trust that He will bring healing and reconciliation in His perfect time. "And the peace of God, which surpasses all understanding, will guard your hearts and minds through Christ Jesus" (Philippians 4:7 NKJV).

Then came another test of faith—a medical report showing abnormal calcification in my breast. Fear tried to creep in. Though the biopsy showed it was benign, my doctor still strongly advised surgery. I had no peace about it. I prayed constantly, asking God for clarity, for wisdom, and to guide my decision. They also wanted me to sign a consent form that would allow student observers during surgery—something I definitely wasn't at peace with. Though I went through the motions of the pre-op process, deep inside, I felt unsettled. I kept seeking God, trusting that if He wanted me to go through with the surgery, He would give me peace.

The day before my scheduled surgery, God spoke clearly, placing a divine roadblock in my path and confirming what I had felt in my heart all along. During my final pre-op exam, the EKG equipment would not work. No matter what they tried, even resetting it and unplugging and plugging it back in, it would not turn on. The technician was baffled. She told me that it was just inspected and had been working fine. My heart jumped! God was telling me to wait and to trust His leading rather than rush forward out of fear or obligation.

That moment reaffirmed these three powerful words: Pray. Trust. Wait. I chose to trust Him. I chose not to move forward with something He was steering me away from. It was a powerful reminder that prayer is not just about speaking to God—it's about listening. Sometimes, His answers come through a deep sense of peace, and other times through circumstances we cannot ignore. Through all of this loss, family struggles, and health concerns, my relationship with Jesus deepened. He taught me to trust Him even when the path is unclear, to wait on Him when I don't have answers, and to rely on prayer not just for comfort but for guidance and direction. Prayer reminds me that I'm not alone, that Jesus is with me and holding my hand, walking on this journey with me. Prayer has strengthened my faith and deepened my understanding of God's amazing grace.

I don't always receive immediate answers, and sometimes waiting is the hardest part, but I believe in the peace that comes with waiting, the quiet reassurance that I am heard. God's timing is always perfect. When I surrender my worries, when I choose to trust instead of control, and when I wait on Him with faith, He never fails me.

Through all the bumps, the ups and downs on this life journey, my relationship with Jesus has grown deeper. He is my Lord and Savior, my comforter, my healer, my provider, my protector, my restorer, and my source of wisdom.

One of the greatest blessings of my prayer journey is being filled with joy and gratitude to walk this journey not alone, but also with the fellowship of my sisters in Christ. Praying together is powerful. We link arms with one another, lift each other up, share burdens, and rejoice in victories. In those moments of shared faith, I see the love of Jesus reflected in them. They constantly remind me, "Sis, we are doing life together."

I'm grateful for my church family. The church is not just a building; it is a place of encouragement, accountability, and strength. In times of uncertainty, their prayers, support, and love remind me that we are never meant to bear our burdens alone. The love of the body of Christ is a gift. We lift each other up as a community of believers. We walk through hardships together, we encourage one another, and we stand in faith together when we are too weary to stand alone.

Prayer isn't just something I do—it is the foundation of my life. Jesus comforts me and heals me, not just physically but also emotionally and spiritually. He sustains me and transforms me in His image. No matter where life takes me, I know I can always return to prayer to find healing, to give and receive forgiveness, and to deepen my relationship with Jesus. Prayer helps me and guides me to navigate through every season, every decision, and every hardship I face. As I seek Jesus and draw near to Him, He will draw near to me. I surrender my fears and find peace in the waiting.

"Draw near to God and He will draw near to you" (James 4:8 NKJV). "And the peace of God, which surpasses all understanding, will guard your hearts and minds through Christ Jesus" (Philippians 4:7 NKJV). I am so thankful to see how far God has brought me. He is so good! He is faithful, and He loves me! "For the Lord is good and his love endures forever; his faithfulness continues through all generations" (Psalm 100:5 NIV).

"God *is* faithful, by whom you were called to the fellowship of His Son, Jesus Christ our Lord" (1 Corinthians 1:9 NKJV). Prayer doesn't always change my circumstances immediately, but it always changes me! Every prayer, whether spoken in tears or gratitude, strengthens my faith and brings me closer to Jesus, revealing that true healing often begins within as He restores the broken places in my heart.

I encourage you to reflect on these three things:

1. How is your prayer life? Are you bringing everything before God in prayer?

2. Do you fully trust God? What areas of your life do you need to surrender to Him?

3. Are you willing to wait on God's timing? How can you develop patience in the waiting season?

After you reflect on these questions, apply these three simple, powerful words: Pray. Trust. Wait.

1-Pray: Seek God in All Things

Prayer is not just about speaking to God but building a relationship with Him. It is where I find strength, guidance, and peace. When life feels unbearable, Jesus is my refuge. In prayer, I can lay down my burdens and find comfort in His presence. "Be anxious for nothing, but in everything by prayer and supplication, with thanksgiving, let your requests be made known to God" (Phillippians 4:6 NKJV). "God *is* our refuge and strength, a very present help in trouble" (Psalm 46:1 NKJV).

2-Trust: Surrender to God's Plan

Trusting God means believing that His ways are higher than ours, even when we don't understand. Let go! And believe in His promises and His plans! Prayer teaches me to surrender my fears and anxieties to Him. God is in control, and He is working all things for my good. "Trust in the Lord with all your heart, and lean not on your own understanding; in all your ways acknowledge Him, and He shall direct your paths" (Proverbs 3:5-6 NKJV). "Cast your burden on the Lord, and He shall sustain you; He shall never permit the righteous to be moved" (Psalm 55:22 NKJV).

3-Wait: God's Timing is Perfect

Waiting on God is an act of faith. His answers come in His perfect time, bringing peace and purpose. It's not easy waiting, but it's in the waiting that faith, patience, and strength grow. "But those who wait on the Lord shall renew *their* strength...they shall run and not be weary, they shall walk and not faint" (Isaiah 40:31 NKJV). "Rest in the Lord, and wait patiently for Him" (Psalm 37:7 NKJV).

My prayer journey continues, and my prayer is that the Lord strengthens your faith and gives you peace. Blessings to you!

About the Author

Best-selling author Isabelle Ramos recently coauthored an anthology, *Sisters Who Pray*, released in April 2025. She also coauthored *Women with Unshakeable Faith* in April 2023.

At a young age, Isabelle discovered her passion for sketching, design, and sewing. Embracing her creative gift, she studied fashion and interior design. After thirty years of fashion merchandising, management, display, and interior design, she opened a gift/antique shop promoting other local artists. Now retired, she resides in Suisun City, California, and is blessed to call Ewa Beach, Hawaii a "second home." Traveling back and forth sparked her entrepreneurial spirit to collaborate with her daughter, Corynna, to launch a business sharing Aloha-inspired jewelry, gifts, and decor.

She served eight years in children's ministry, teaching "The Fruit of the Spirit", etiquette, and Sunday Bible classes. As a prayer warrior, she loves spending devotional time with Jesus and fellowshipping/sharing with her "Sisters." She enjoys fun times with her grand-girls, baking, being creative in arts and crafts, and sharing the joy of knowing Jesus!

She and her husband of fifty-two years, Anthony, have four children, ten grandchildren, and two great-grandchildren.

Connect with Isabelle

- Email: inspired1000@gmail.com

- IG: www.Instagram.com/passion4healthweath

- Facebook: <u>www.facebook.com/Isabel</u> <u>leNifalarRamos</u>

The Power of PRAYER—In the Midst of the Storm!

Dr. Lisa Yvette Jones

April, my birth month, 2009, I decided to give myself the gift of health. It was that yearly appointment we ladies dread but know we must keep—the Pap smear. It is a non-negotiable act of self-care that can save our life.

What I thought would be a routine appointment turned into a whirlwind of tests and consultations. Before I knew it, I had two ob-gyn appointments that turned into two appointments with gynecologic oncologists: yes, cancer specialists.

Nothing could have been more disconcerting than to hear, "Ms. Jones, you have been diagnosed with stage three cervical cancer, papillary serous carcinoma of the cervix. It is high grade and quite aggressive, to the point that it is spreading."

Immediate denial was followed by total shock. My mind raced to recall any women diagnosed with cancer in my family; there were none. I couldn't comprehend how cancer could grow inside me when I had no familial history. I had absolutely no symptoms, no irregularities, nothing. How could this diagnosis be?

As any intelligent person would do, I asked tons of questions, conducted independent research, and prayed. Through my questioning, I discovered weight was one of the main precursors to the cancer diagnosis—at that time, I weighed 362 pounds. The Centers for Disease Control (CDC) reports that 40% of cancers in America are related to obesity. While not everyone who is obese will develop cancer, science has shown a clear link between obesity and at least thirteen types of cancers in the United States alone.

Despite the urgency of my diagnosis and the need to have surgery as soon as possible, according to the medical doctors, I told the doctors I needed time. They warned me that if I did not have surgery within days—no later than a week—I would certainly die. From their experience, that type of cancer spread quickly, and once attached to a major organ, surgery would no longer be an option. I heard them; however, I insisted that I needed time to consult with my Chief Physician and medical team—the Father, Son, and Holy Spirit. I was already activating my faith. If God's Word stood true, then I was already healed and made whole by the stripes of Jesus. I chose to believe God's Word. "And with his stripes we are healed" (Isaiah 53:5 KJV).

This was a storm. I needed to send out a strategic SOS known as the Power of Prayer. My first call was to my ex-husband, the father of our only son, Anthony Maurice Jones, II. Compassionate and unwavering, he assured me, "We will get through this as a family. Don't worry. I will be with you through this." Pause for a second and allow that to sink in. When my now-late ex-husband and I separated and then divorced, I prayed and asked God to make me a better woman, and not a bitter woman. He did! Praise God, and we were great co-parents. We remained friends until his untimely transition in 2016. We had to because our son absolutely loved and honored his father, and he was exceptionally close to him. His father loved and cherished him more.

I then called Mother Laura Heard—everyone needs a dragon-slaying, bringing-heaven-to-earth, fasting prayer warrior like Mother Laura Heard in their life—and reached out to other prayer warriors whom I trusted to know the words and the worth of prayer without spreading my business before I was ready to share the news. This was crucial because our dear mother, the now late and great Queenie Victoria Thompson, had just returned home from rehabilitating for two months from a mild stroke. I could not bring myself to share my diagnosis with her, not until I had all the facts. I knew how much my mother loved me, and I did not want to trigger another stroke. She sacrificed so much for us as a single parent of seven children. I didn't tell Anthony, either. He was studying for his ninth-grade finals at a prestigious boarding school, Cranbrook-Kingswood High School in Bloomfield Hills, MI, and I did not want to disrupt his studies. I know, I was concerned about everyone else while dealing with deadly news about my own life. Nevertheless, I had a strategy.

Knowing my community of support helped me navigate that storm. It is imperative to surround yourself with people who will stand in faith with you when facing a storm. "For where two or three gather in my name, there I am with them" (Matthew 18:20 NIV).

Understanding the importance of sharing this information with at least one sibling, I told my brother, Duane. As difficult as it was for him to see our mother daily and temporarily carry my secret, it was the best option until I was ready to reveal the news to my entire immediate family, including Anthony and my goddaughter, Brandi Rochae.

I went on a three-day fast—no water, no food. I prayerfully joined my faith with theirs, but I also knew that I had to believe in the power of Whom I was praying to and with the expectation that His Word remained truthful. "And without faith it is impossible to please him, for whoever would draw near to God must believe that he exists and that he rewards those who seek him" (Hebrews 11:6 ESV). It was time to activate my strategic SOS plan. After ministering to others through their storms, I needed to minister to myself.

- **S:** Shut out all distractions and negative thoughts that distort my thinking. I prayed over healing scriptures and God's promises for my complete healing and wholeness in body, mind, and spirit.

- **O:** Open my heart to hear God's voice and bask in His divine presence. I removed all obstacles that would bombard my thoughts that did not align with God's Word.

- **S:** Shelter in my prayer closet, pouring out my fears, standing on my faith, and trusting in an unfailing and unwavering God.

I remained sheltered in place until the storm passed. On the third day, while praying, I heard the words, "It is not unto death. You shall live and not die, and this will never return again."

I rejoiced in a shout, a praise that awakened my entire neighborhood. I knew at that moment, the spreading of cancer had ceased, and I was healed. With renewed faith, I returned to the oncologist and informed him what my Heavenly Father had revealed to me through the power of my prayers. It was mid-May 2009 when I declared to the doctors that I would have the surgery on June 29, 2009—over a month later—despite his dire warnings.

The doctor was incredulous and told me that I was one stubborn patient. I said, "No, doc, as your partner in my health, I am one steadfast patient."

He agreed, saying, "I will see you on June twenty-ninth."

"Yes, you will."

I had to stand firm on what I knew to be true for the One that I trust. "But Jesus turned him about, and when he saw her, he said, Daughter, be of good comfort; thy faith hath made thee whole" (Matthew 9:22 KJV). Hallelujah!

June 29, 2009, the surgery was successful, and here I am today, cancer-free and celebrating each anniversary as a victorious milestone. The doctors may have given me a diagnosis and two death sentences, but my chief physician, my Heavenly Father, gave me a prognosis to live and not die!

Prayer is the best place to position ourselves when life bombards us with trials beyond our physical control and without notice. We need a strategy to anchor our soul and guard our peace—my six-step process of the Power of PRAYER, which encapsulates the transformative power that carried me through my storm:

P — <u>P</u>eace: God's peace, which surpasses all understanding, guarded my heart and mind. It lifted my fears and worries, leaving me in a space of tranquility beyond human comprehension.

R — <u>R</u>eset and <u>R</u>esist Catastrophizing over the Storm: Prayer allowed me to reset my thinking and perspective. It was a time to recognize that God was ordering my steps and that I needed to align my will with His. No one chooses to be in a storm; however, when we trust the One who anchors us in His care during the storm, we begin to see ourselves victoriously on the other side of it.

A — <u>A</u>lign: Just as a car requires proper alignment to drive straight, prayer aligned my will with God's perfect will. It positioned me to walk the straight and narrow path, guided by His wisdom and His Word.

Y — <u>Y</u>ield to God in Prayer: I surrendered all my fears and trusted Him with all my heart. That gift brought clarity and peace. I did not have the answers, but I trusted the One who is my answer.

E — Expectation: I approached God in prayer with the expectation that He would hear and answer according to His will. This expectation fortified my faith and gave me the strength to stand firm that I was healed well before the surgery. After my three-day fast, I saw myself on the other side of the ugliness plaguing me. My expectations are always in God.

R — Restorative Refuge: Prayer is restorative, renewing strength and vigor. It replaced my fear with faith and my despair with trust. The enemy would have us operate in fear. The power of prayer restores our faith and trust in God regardless of what we may experience. The Word of God teaches us that His way is perfect, His word is flawless, and He shields all who take refuge in Him (Psalm 18:30 NIV). I knew that if I wanted a safe place, it was in community and in communion with God first.

The power of prayer fills our cup to overflowing. Our full cup is for us, and we serve others from our overflow. As for me, cancer was put on notice and forever canceled! The power of my strategic SOS and PRAYER carried me through the storm, restored my body and spirit, and continued to be my guiding force. Whatever storm you are facing, know that the same power of prayer is available to you.

I leave you with the words of a hymnal, in part, "What a Friend We have in Jesus," written by Joseph M. Scriven in 1855 as a poem of comfort to his mother. "O what peace we often forfeit. O, what needless pains we bear. All because we do not carry, everything to God in prayer."

Dear friend, know that the power of prayer is your license to bring the power of heaven into your earthly situation. Do you recall that I was almost four hundred pounds when diagnosed? Since that time, I have released over two hundred pounds! God did His part in restoring my health. It was up to me to do my part. I praise God for being forever healed, healthy, and full of life. Stand firm in your faith and watch God navigate you to victory, too.

About the Author

Dr. Lisa Yvette Jones is a nine-time best-selling author, orator, success enthusiast, and the chief caring officer (CCO) and founder of iC.A.R.E. Leadership, LLC, a coaching practice focused on transforming professional leadership. With years of experience in leadership development, coaching, mentoring, and counseling, Lisa inspires career professionals to prioritize self-care, embrace personal growth, and find purpose in their work.

Her leadership expertise has earned her global recognition, including sharing the stage with Dr. Les Brown at the Power Voice Summit, being featured in *Women of Dignity Magazine* as one of the Top 50 Women to Watch in Leadership, and serving as a panelist for the United Nations Women's Economic Thumbprint. She's received numerous awards for her dedicated leadership and team-building success.

A John Maxwell certified coach and Dale Carnegie-trained speaker, Lisa has completed advanced training from the Les Brown Power Voice Academy, Sage Lavine's Women Rocking Business Leadership Academy, and more. She holds a BA in business administration, an MA in counseling, and an honorary PhD in business administration. Lisa believes compassionate leadership is the key to reducing employee turnover and creating thriving, purpose-driven workplaces.

Connect with Dr. Lisa

- LisaYvetteJones.com

- LisaYvetteJones@gmail.com

Before I Let Go: Praying My Way Out of Depression

Duania K. Hall

"You have permission to say exactly what you need to say out loud."

That's what I told myself as I lay face flat on my living room floor, cheeks and clothes soaked from endless tears. I wondered if my tears had informed God of my pain because

I was not okay. Kirk Franklin's "More Than I Can Bear" blasted from the speakers. I didn't know if this was meant to encourage me or mock me, but at that moment, I had reached my limit.

I made it to my fifties bearing a lot of things. From my history of "keep on keeping on" after trauma, I was seen as the strong one. But I lay on the floor, blending into the gray and black carpet, desperately needing relief from the depression greeting me. Depression had visited me before, but this time, it brought extra bags for an extended stay. To say I was looking for a miracle and a way out is an understatement. I cried out to the Lord. "I'm tired, Lord! I can't keep living like this! I want to get everything set up for my kids and position them to be able to take care of each other. Help me prepare a good table for them, and then just let me go!"

Have you ever felt like you wanted to throw your hands up and say, "I'm done"? Not done with a moment or a conversation, but done trying and done waiting for things to get better? There are blocks of time when life gets hard. Sometimes, this lasts a few days or a few weeks, and sometimes, it lasts for months or even years.

By the third month of depression's visit, feelings of responsibility for so many things that happened, and even things that didn't happen, weighed me down. Did I navigate becoming a widow correctly as my son tried to fill the void of not having a dad? Health issues left me with so little energy I'd often be wiped out before nine a.m. I couldn't avoid the things that needed to be fixed around the house, yet I had no means to fix them. I was still processing a breakup with a man I cared deeply for.

With over 50% of my hair being gray, I struggled to accept myself. I no longer enjoyed my mirror dates as light and dark spots invaded various parts of my body, including my face.

Having been blessed with flawless skin, beautiful brown hair, and the energy to dance the night away, I began to understand why people resorted to fat-freezing techniques to perfect their bodies—my fat stuck with me like a sorority sister. What was happening to me? I felt like I was falling apart and might become a burden to my kids. This was devastating! I needed God to pop out and show me something new because my desire to hold on had nearly worn out.

My kids were simultaneously going through tough times, and I tried to show up for them, though I didn't have the capacity to show up for anything anymore. During my seventh month of depression, I wondered if God would just leave me to fend for myself. Why did I still feel this way? I asked God, "Why are you allowing this? What do you want from me? How low do you need me to go? I am literally on the floor."

Some of you might be thinking, "Girl, you were venting, not praying," or "You talk to God like that?" Well, He is all-knowing, so He already knows exactly what I'm thinking. And at that moment, I needed to say exactly what I needed to say out loud, perhaps with a few cuss words. But God knows my heart; it was breaking. I felt lost and unrecognizable. I thought my suffering would never end.

When God is reshaping you or positioning you for your next moves, it can be an "ugly cry" process. Prayer might be gritty, not pretty. When we're in the midst of our storms, it's hard to hold on, but right at the point when you think your prayers are getting stuck in Heaven's queue and not reaching God, an act of resurrection occurs. "Weeping may endure for a night, but joy cometh in the morning" (Psalm 30:5 KJV).

I cried night after night. Then one day, I woke up with what I call "God Tap," urging me to reach out to a specific person; we'll call her

Miss Angel. I didn't have her number, but I called someone who did. They texted me the number in thirty seconds flat, so I knew Jesus was on the main line and my call was getting through. I called Miss Angel, and she answered on the second ring.

"Hey, Duania, how are you doing?"

I had no words, just tears.

"What's going on, sis?"

"I'm depressed, and I can't shake it. I cry every day. I struggle to get out of bed every morning. My body is going through changes I don't understand, and I feel like I'm falling apart. I don't recognize myself anymore. My speaking engagements are not coming, and I feel useless on this earth. I don't want to be here anymore."

"Oh, no, sis, don't say that! I rebuke that! We're going to pray right now."

We prayed for about an hour. Miss Angel was not playing that day, nor any day after that. She called to check on me and sent inspirational texts, scriptures, and prayers every single day. "Now to him who is able to do immeasurably more than all we ask or imagine, according to his power that is at work within us" (Ephesians 3:20 NIV). On my lowest days, Miss Angel went into full-blown prayer-warrior mode, praying for me like I was one of her own children. She would not let me go, and she wanted me to know that God wouldn't either.

Miss Angel walked this unimaginably hard road with me for months. And in November, I ran into her at a mutual friend's party. It was the first time I had been out of the house to socialize since my depression battle started. We hugged each other tight, and I told her, "You saved my life."

"Our Father in Heaven knows what we're going through, and He will always send other faithful warriors to our rescue so that we may know we are not alone. I was just the one He sent to you, although many were unseen."

I had been praying for God to send help for over a year and thought it would never come, or not in the way I believed it should. Before I let go, God sent Miss Angel to be strong for me.

Shortly after Christmas, a friend of mine texted. *Hey girl, you've been real quiet in the group chat and we haven't really seen you all year. Are you okay?*

I replied, *No, I'm not okay, but I will be.*

She empathized with what I was going through, let me know she was there if I needed to talk, and invited me to brunch on January 1. Some people we went to school with get together every year on New Year's Day and have brunch at the same restaurant, WeHo Bistro. I accepted her invitation. I remember standing in the restaurant doorway, giving myself a pep talk and taking a deep breath because, after what I had been through, socializing was a big task.

I walked in looking fabulous in black velvet pants and a white sweater, cut on the shoulders and lined with rhinestones. Everyone greeted and hugged me. I sat, then the host asked me to pray. Still feeling emotionally fragile, I wondered if I was qualified to do this. But I have never passed on an opportunity to pray. The little pastor in me took over. I instructed everyone to stand and hold their neighbors' hands. Then I began. "Lord, you know it has been a rough year."

"Oooh, girl, yes it has!"

I listed familiar struggles as God laid them out for me, and echoes of agreement accompanied each one. Next, I named all the things to be thankful for. I hadn't been sure I'd make it to the New Year, yet there I was, in a room full of good people and an opportunity to fellowship. I ended the prayer with my favorite line. "Lord, bless this food and the hands that prepared it. Let it make us thick and not sick, in Jesus' name." And as the Amen corner evolved, so did my gratitude. I was glad that I hadn't let go.

I have been praying all my life, but that depression hit different. God answered my prayer for help and sent me another sistah, who prayed to help me get through it. And I learned some valuable lessons from this process.

- Find a healing affirmation and say it every day through the depression. Don't be afraid of the changes that occur because of it.

- Pray without subconsciously telling God how to answer it; otherwise, you can delay parts of your healing.

- Pray honestly; don't avoid prayer because you hold God responsible for your pain. Confront Him and know that He understands, He cares, and He gives you permission to say exactly what you need to say out loud.

- Don't get stuck on who you think should help you on this journey. People you don't expect may be sent to help you, but your eyes are wide shut.

- Journaling through depression provides a safe space for releasing overwhelming feelings. Journaling also serves as a reminder of how you got through the situation.

- Lastly, claim your deliverance; speak to your storms through scripture and prayers

To help you with this, here's one of the prayers Miss Angel texted me during my battle with depression:

Good Morning Prayer.

Father, thank You for another day. I don't know what this day might bring. Therefore, I put my trust in You. Fill me with Your peace—the peace that surpasses all understanding. Cover me with Your presence and comfort my mind. Give me a fresh mental and spiritual attitude. Cause me to rest and not be stressed. Let the rivers of joy and happiness fill me every moment of this day. In the mighty name of Jesus, I pray, Amen.

Sistahs, I love you with the love of God. I am praying for you, I am rooting for you, and please, never let go!

About the Author

Duania Hall is a motivational speaker whose poetic style and raw storytelling have captivated audiences around the world. Affectionately called the Whole Woman Coach, Duania uses her background in social work to empower women to thrive after trauma and take charge of their destinies. As the founder of Poetic Dezigns, she aims to create a unique experience for her clients and provide them with prolific speakers and poets for all occasions.

Connect with Duania

- Website: www.poeticdezigns.com

- Email: poeticdezigns@gmail.com

I Am Purposeful: Walking Through the Process of Life

Cassandra Hayes

Have you ever faced a challenge so unforeseen, so overwhelming, that it crippled you with fear? A moment where you truly believed this could be the end? I have. I questioned everything: Why was this happening, why now, and why me? I didn't understand, but even in my confusion, I clung to faith. I held on to prayer, God's promises, and His

Word. And through it all, God's unfailing hand guided, shielded, and protected me.

This chapter is a testimony of how God carried me through two of my life's darkest, most terrifying times. A time when hope felt distant and I thought I had reached the end of my journey. When calamity came knocking at my door, uninvited and unwelcome, bringing fear, doubt, and uncertainty, I had a choice. Would I crumble, or would I stand?

What do you do when you're at your lowest, weak and helpless, and the very people you call on for help dismiss your cries and leave you for dead? I learned firsthand the power of prayer— prayer changes things!

"Confess your faults one to another, and pray one for another, that ye may be healed. The effectual fervent prayer of a righteous man availeth much" (James 5:16 KJV).

I remember that day as if it was yesterday. My routine was the same: work, pick up my daughter, make sure her homework was done, and get her ready for bed. Nothing out of the ordinary. No signs, no warnings. Just another day. But the next morning, everything changed. I woke up in excruciating pain—pain I couldn't describe, pain that took my breath away. Still, being a mother, I pressed through, determined to get my daughter off to school. But something in my spirit told me to keep her home. As the pain intensified, fear crept in. I didn't know what was happening to me, but I knew it wasn't normal.

Intrusive thoughts flooded my mind. What if I don't make it? What will happen to my daughter? But even in fear, I prayed. I declared, "God, You didn't bring me this far to leave me." Barely able to stand, I called 911.

When the paramedics arrived, I expected help. What I received instead was a harsh intrusion into my home. A female paramedic barked orders at my daughter, demanding she turn off the TV. How dare she? This was my home, my safe space, and here she was, overstepping. But I was too weak to respond, too weak to fight back. They examined me and refused to take me to the hospital because my daughter couldn't ride with me due to her age. Instead, they suggested I "find a ride." Imagine that! Calling for help, and the ones sent to help me dismissing my pain.

At that moment, I could have given up. I could have let fear and anger consume me. But I chose prayer. My friend wasn't available, but she called another friend, who drove across town to get me. By the time I made it to her car, I was slumped over in pain, barely holding on. Upon arriving at the hospital, everything happened fast. The doctors ran tests, gave me pain relief, and soon delivered the news! My appendix had ruptured. I needed emergency surgery.

Facing my greatest fear, panic set in. At seven years old, I witnessed my baby sister, just two years younger than me, die from the same condition. She woke up early one morning, asked for water, went back to sleep, and never woke up again. That moment had burned into my memory, and there I was, facing the same fate. I was terrified. My mind told me this was it. But prayer told me otherwise.

I prayed. My sisters in Christ covered me in prayer. I held on to God's Word even when fear tried to take hold. And God did what only He can do.

The surgery was successful. While I was in recovery, the doctor spoke to two of my sister's friends, one of whom was a nurse, and told them something that still shakes me to this day. "The only reason she's alive is because of the fatty tissue in her stomach. It stopped the poison from spreading to her vital organs." The very thing I once criticized about my body, the extra weight I often complained about, saved my life. I broke down and praised God for fatty tissue! Because in that moment, I knew without a shadow of a doubt that God was my healer.

Years later, during the pandemic, I faced another life-threatening experience. I contracted COVID-19. It started with a sore throat, but each day, my condition worsened. By day three, I knew home remedies wouldn't be enough. Fear loomed over me. I had already lost three family members to COVID. I was weak, barely able to breathe or stand. With hospitals overwhelmed, I called the nurse's line. After assessing me, the nurse urged me to call 911 immediately. When the paramedics arrived, I expected help, but history repeated itself. Despite my weakness, loss of appetite, and clear signs of distress, including untouched bowls of soup on my counter, the paramedic insisted I had the flu and was "at the end of it." He refused to take me to the hospital, claiming it was for my own protection. Once again, I found myself abandoned when I needed help the most.

And once again, I turned to the one source of strength that had never failed me—prayer.

The next day, I struggled to get up, literally rolling onto the floor because I didn't have the strength to stand on my own. It took me nearly an hour just to get dressed. But I was determined. I had to make it to the urgent care, even if I had to go alone. Who could I have called without putting them at risk? Those were uncertain times, the early days of COVID when fear and isolation had gripped the world. I mustered up just enough strength to make it to my car, barely sitting upright as I drove. Thank God the urgent care wasn't far from my home. I don't remember how I made it inside, but I did. When the doctor walked into the room, his eyes filled with concern. He saw me slumped over and knew right away that my condition was serious. "I'm going to take care of you and get you better," he said.

I felt instant relief and silently thanked my Lord and Savior—Jesus. The doctor tested me for COVID. Though the results wouldn't be available for a few days, he prescribed multiple medications. I don't know how I made it to the pharmacy, but God gave me just enough strength to do what I needed. A few days later, my test results confirmed what I already knew, I had COVID. But by then, my healing journey had already begun. As I took the prescribed medication, I started feeling better each day. And with every bit of progress, I praised Jesus, my Lord and Savior. Each day, I declared, "If He did it before, He will do it again!" I held on to the truth that God had healed me before, and He was healing me again.

Looking back, I see how each trial, each challenge, and each storm strengthened me. Even when I was at my lowest. Even when I was weak and abandoned. Even when I thought I wouldn't make it. God was with me. He never left me. He never forsook me. He healed me, He carried me, and He reminded me that I am purposeful.

"And we know that all things work together for good to them that love God, to them who are the called according to his purpose" (Romans 8:28 KJV).

I learned that:

- God is a protector, even when we don't see it. The paramedics abandoned me, but God had already made a way.

- Prayer is powerful. Even when fear grips you, pray. Even when doubt creeps in, pray.

- We may not always understand the why, but we can trust the Who. God is sovereign, and His plan is greater than our understanding.

All of this reminded me that I am purposeful. Every trial, every storm, every setback only positioned me for greater.

If you are facing a storm today, hold on. If you are feeling abandoned, know that God is with you. If you are struggling with fear, doubt, or uncertainty, turn to prayer. God has not forgotten you, and He will bring you through!

Let this testimony serve as a reminder that God still answers prayers. He still works miracles. And even when we don't understand, He is still working all things together for our good.

About the Author

Cassandra Hayes was born and raised in Brooklyn, NY. She is a first-time best-selling coauthor of the anthology *Her Unbreakable Spirit* and a second-time author who coauthored *Sisters Who Pray*, released in April 2025. Cassandra holds a bachelor of arts degree and a certificate in human resource management from Southern New Hampshire University.

She is the CEO of Cee's Heavenly Boutique, LLC, where her passion for fashion intersects with her commitment to social change.

With over a decade of advocacy in mental health and domestic violence, she is certified through NAMI In Our Own Voice and Sharing Hope. She also holds a certification in mental health first aid for both youth and adults. She believes deeply in the transformative power of compassion, inspired by one of Maya Angelou's Quotes: "I've learned that people will forget what you said, people will forget what you did, but people will never forget how you made them feel." Her fervent commitment to raising awareness underscores her multifaceted approach to empowerment. Through her work, Cassandra inspires countless individuals to conquer adversity and create a lasting impact on the world.

Connect with Cassandra

- Website: ceesheavenlyboutique.com

- Facebook: Cassandra Hayes

SISTERS WHO PRAY

A Final Call to Prayer, Unity, and Deeper Spiritual Engagement

As we come to the closing pages of this powerful collection of prayers, testimonies, and reflections, let us be reminded that prayer is more than words—it is a way of life. It is our sacred connection to God and a lifeline for those we stand in the gap for.

This final section is an invitation to go deeper—not just to read about prayer, but to actively engage in it. To intercede boldly, uplift one another, and remain steadfast in faith.

The Word of God reminds us in **1 Thessalonians 5:17 (KJV),** *"Pray without ceasing."* This is not just a suggestion but a divine call to a lifestyle of continual prayer, communion, and faith in action.

Sisters, let us rise as women of prayer—unwavering, unshaken, and united in spirit. When we pray, heaven moves. And together, we become a force that cannot be ignored.

So, don't stop here. Keep reading. Let these final pages stir your faith, challenge your spirit, and remind you of the power you hold when you pray. There's more ahead—prayers to declare, truths to embrace, and a call to action that will equip you for the journey ahead.

Because victory belongs to those who pray.

And before you close this book, we invite you to continue this journey with us. **Check out our other powerful collaborations**—books that inspire, uplift, and equip women of faith to walk boldly in their purpose.

We also invite you to experience a deeper level of **restoration and renewal at the Proverbs 31 Wellness Retreat.** This **luxurious, faith-filled retreat** is designed to help women reset their **mind, body, and spirit** in a sacred and refreshing environment.

Through **spirit-led empowerment sessions, biblical teachings, and holistic wellness experiences,** this retreat is an opportunity to step away from the noise and truly reconnect with God's plan for your life.

Join us for **fellowship, spiritual growth, and divine rest** in a space where faith and wellness meet.

Visit to learn more, reserve your spot, and stay connected with our community.

Your journey doesn't end here—this is just the beginning.

Prayers of Faith: Shaping Your Future

Sis, your prayers are not just about the present moment. They are about shaping your future. They are seeds you plant today that will grow and flourish tomorrow. When you pray in faith, you align yourself with God's divine plan for your life, and His will begins to unfold in ways you can't even imagine.

It's easy to think that prayer is just about asking God for what we need. But true prayer, the kind of prayer that moves mountains, is rooted in faith—faith that God will answer according to His will and His timing.

In Matthew 21:22, Jesus tells us, "If you believe, you will receive whatever you ask for in prayer." That's the power of faith-filled prayer. When you approach God with a heart full of trust and expectation, you position yourself for a breakthrough.

But here's the thing: it's not just about praying for what you need in the moment—it's about speaking life over your future. It's about declaring God's promises over your destiny, your dreams, your family, and your ministry.

When you pray, you're not just changing your present circumstances—you're prophesying your future. You're laying the groundwork for the breakthroughs to come, the doors that will open, and the victory that's already yours in Christ.

Your prayers matter. They have the power to break generational curses, heal old wounds, and bring forth new opportunities. Your prayers are the blueprint for the future that God has already designed for you.

So don't just pray for today's struggles—pray for your future. Declare what God has spoken over your life, and trust that He is faithful to fulfill His promises. As you continue to pray, know that you are building the foundation for a future full of blessings, joy, and purpose.

Pray with vision. Pray with faith. And watch how God transforms your life, one prayer at a time.

Declaration

I declare that my prayers shape my future, align my life with God's divine plan, and bring forth the breakthroughs, blessings, and purpose He has designed for me. I trust His timing and His will, and I walk in faith, knowing that He is faithful to fulfill His promises.

Dr. Paulette Harper

THE POWER OF SISTERHOOD IN PRAYER

Sis, there is something incredibly powerful about praying together. When we come together in agreement, it's as though the heavens open up even wider. A cord of three strands is not easily broken (Ecclesiastes 4:12), and there's a special kind of strength that rises when sisters stand together in prayer.

In the book of Acts, we see the early church come together in prayer and unity, and the result was a mighty outpouring of the Holy Spirit. Acts 12:5 tells us that while Peter was in prison, the church prayed earnestly for him. In response to their collective prayers, God sent an angel to release him! There is power in corporate prayer—power that can break chains, open doors, and set people free.

When you pray alone, it's powerful. But when you pray with your sisters, there is an explosive power that God honors. There is something special about being in a community where your prayer life is uplifted, where you're supported, and where your faith is ignited.

Sisters, we weren't meant to carry burdens alone. There's a reason why God calls us to fellowship and to pray with and for one another. When we stand in the gap for our sisters, we're not just lifting them up—we're also strengthening ourselves.

In times of joy and in times of sorrow, prayer becomes a shared experience. When you stand alongside another woman, interceding for her, you're not just offering words—you're offering love, compassion, and faith. You're showing her that she's not alone in her struggles. You're reinforcing the belief that God is moving on her behalf.

Let's commit to being a sisterhood that prays for one another. Let's encourage each other to pray boldly, to pray often, and to never give up.

Because when we pray together, we become a force to be reckoned with.

Declaration

I declare that the power of prayer unites us as sisters. I commit to standing in the gap for my sisters, knowing that our prayers are powerful and effective. I will pray boldly, I will pray often, and I will never give up. Together, we are a force that shakes heaven, breaks chains, and brings forth break-throughs. I declare that when we pray together, we will see the mighty hand of God move in our lives and the lives of those we lift up in prayer. Amen.

Dr. Paulette Harper

When Women Pray, Things Shift

Sis, don't ever underestimate the power of your prayers. When women pray, things shift. Doors open, strongholds break, and the enemy has no choice but to back down. A woman who knows how to pray is a woman who walks in victory.

In the Bible, women have always been at the forefront of powerful prayers that moved heaven. Deborah prayed and rose up as a leader who delivered Israel from oppression

(Judges 4:4-7). Ruth prayed with unwavering faith and commitment, and God led her to a place of divine favor and purpose, becoming part of the lineage of Jesus Christ (Ruth 1:16-17, Matthew 1:5). Anna prayed in the temple day and night, and through her prayers, she was among the first to witness the arrival of the Savior (Luke 2:36-38).

These weren't just ordinary prayers—they were bold, faith-filled, and relentless. They were the kind of prayers that refused to accept "no" as the final answer. And that same power lives in you.

The enemy would love for you to think that your prayers don't matter. That your voice isn't heard. That nothing is changing. But let me remind you—he is a liar. Your prayers are shaking things in the spirit. Even when you don't see it, God is working behind the scenes.

But here's the key: You can't stop praying.

Too many times, we get discouraged when we don't see immediate results. We pray once, maybe twice, and when things don't shift instantly, we start doubting. But sis, prayer is a weapon, not a wish list. It's a declaration of faith. It's warfare. And just like in any battle, persistence is key.

So, pray until the chains break. Pray until the healing manifests. Pray until the doors open. Pray until you see the shift. And even after the breakthrough comes, keep praying.

Because when women pray, heaven responds.

Declaration

I declare that my prayers are powerful and effective. I will not be discouraged by delays or doubts. I will pray boldly, with persistence and faith, knowing that heaven is responding. I stand firm in the power of prayer, knowing that every prayer moves mountains, breaks chains, and brings forth breakthrough. I commit to being relentless in prayer, declaring victory in Jesus' name. Amen.

Dr. Paulette Harper

SISTERS WHO STAND IN THE GAP

One of the greatest gifts of a praying sisterhood is knowing that you don't have to carry the weight of life alone. When women of faith come together in prayer, miracles happen. Chains break, healing flows, and heaven responds.

Sis, let me remind you—your prayers aren't just for you. There is someone connected to your obedience. Someone is depending on you to intercede. Someone needs your strength when they feel weak. We were never meant to walk this faith journey alone, and that's why the power of standing in the gap for one another is so vital.

Moses had Aaron and Hur to hold up his arms when he grew weary in battle (Exodus 17:12). Ruth had Naomi to guide her into purpose. Mary had Elizabeth to confirm what God was doing in her life. Who do you have? And more importantly, who can count on you?

Sisters, we are called to pray for one another—not just with a quick "I'll pray for you" and then forget, but with intentional, fervent prayer. When one of us is hurting, we all feel it. When one of us is struggling, we rally together. When one of us is in need, we storm heaven's gates until the answer comes.

It's easy to say we'll pray for someone, but let's take it further. Let's show up. Let's be present. Let's listen. Let's send that text, make that phone call, and be the kind of sisters who don't just pray, but pray until something happens.

When we stand in the gap, we become the hands and feet of Jesus. We remind our sisters that they are not alone, that they are seen, and that God is still moving on their behalf.

So, let's make a commitment. Let's be the sisters who pray. The sisters who intercede, uplift, and encourage. The sisters who hold each other up when life gets heavy. The sisters who remind each other that no battle is fought alone.

Because when we stand in the gap, victory is inevitable.

Declaration

I declare that I will be a sister who stands in the gap. I will not only pray for others, but I will also show up, be present, and intercede with intentionality. I will be a source of strength and encouragement, uplifting my sisters when they are weak. I believe that when we stand in the gap together, victory is guaranteed. I commit to walking alongside others in prayer, knowing that no one fights alone. In Jesus' name, Amen.

Dr. Paulette Harper

PRAY, SIS, PRAY

There is something undeniably powerful about women coming together in prayer. When sisters unite—lifting their voices in intercession, standing in the gap for one another, and believing for breakthroughs—heaven responds. There is no competition in the Kingdom, only collaboration. No jealousy, only joy. No division, only divine alignment.

Sisters, we were never meant to walk this faith journey alone. The enemy thrives in isolation, but we thrive in community. There is strength in knowing that when life becomes overwhelming, we have a circle of praying women who will war in the spirit on our behalf. We need sisters who don't just say, "I'll pray for you," but who will stop everything and pray right then and there. Sisters who will bombard heaven until the chains break. Women who will intercede until something shifts.

Have you ever felt the power of someone truly praying for you? Not just a quick mention but an intentional, fervent, fire-filled prayer? That kind of prayer moves mountains. That kind of prayer stirs the atmosphere and shifts destinies. That kind of prayer is what *Sisters Who Pray* is all about.

God has given us an assignment—to pray without ceasing, to cover our families, to intercede for nations, and to be the watch-women on the wall. When we pray together, we create a force that hell cannot withstand.

I challenge you today—who are your prayer sisters? Who is in your corner, covering you in prayer as much as you cover them? If you don't have a circle yet, pray for one. If you already do, treasure them.

Declaration

Today, I take my rightful place as a praying woman. I declare that I am a warrior in the spirit, standing in unity with my sisters. No weapon formed against us shall prosper. We are covered, strengthened, and empowered by the Holy Spirit. Our prayers shake the heavens, break chains, and release divine breakthroughs. Together, we stand. Together, we pray. Together, we win. In Jesus' name, Amen.

Dr. Paulette Harper

Praying Through the Storm

Storms in life are inevitable. At some point, we all face challenges that shake us to our core—sickness, loss, financial struggles, broken relationships, or seasons of uncertainty. It's easy to pray when everything is going well, but what about when life gets hard? What about when your faith is tested? What about when the storm is raging, and it feels like God is silent?

This is where prayer becomes our anchor.

In Mark 4:39, when Jesus was in the boat with His disciples and a fierce storm arose, He simply spoke: "Peace, be still." And immediately, the storm obeyed. But before Jesus calmed the storm, the disciples panicked. They were afraid, wondering why He wasn't doing something. How often do we do the same? We face a trial, and instead of resting in the truth that God is with us, we let fear take over.

But here's what I want you to remember, sis: If Jesus is in your boat, you will not sink. The storm may be fierce, the waves may be high, and the winds may be howling, but you are not alone. Your prayers are not in vain. Even when you can't see the breakthrough, keep praying. Even when it feels like the storm will never end, keep believing.

There is power in praying through the storm. Prayer is not just about asking God to change the situation—it's about allowing Him to change us in the process. Sometimes, the storm doesn't pass immediately because God is strengthening us in the middle of it. He's building our endurance, stretching our faith, and teaching us how to trust Him on a deeper level.

And here's the beauty of having praying sisters in your life—you don't have to face the storm alone. There is strength in numbers. When your faith feels weak, let your sisters intercede for you. When your voice shakes, let them declare the Word over your life. When you feel like you're drowning, let them remind you that God is still in control.

Sis, this storm will not take you out. You are stronger than you think. Your prayers are reaching heaven. And just like Jesus spoke to the winds and the waves, peace is coming. Hold on. Keep praying. Your breakthrough is on the way.

Declaration

Today, I stand firm in my faith. I declare that no storm will shake my foundation, for God is my anchor. I will not fear the winds or the waves, because I know that Jesus is in my boat. I am stronger than I realize, and I will rise above every trial. My prayers are powerful, and heaven is responding. I trust that God is working in the midst of the storm, building my endurance and strengthening my faith. I declare that peace is coming, and my breakthrough is on the horizon. In Jesus' name, Amen.

Dr. Paulette Harper

THE POWER OF
PRAYING BOLDLY

Too often, we pray small prayers because we are afraid to ask God for big things. We whisper timid requests instead of declaring His promises with authority. But sis, let me remind you—we serve a BIG God! A God who parts seas, heals the sick, raises the dead, and provides in ways that don't even make sense.

Hebrews 4:16 tells us to "come boldly to the throne of grace"—not timidly, not fearfully, but boldly! That means we don't have to approach God like beggars. We are His daughters. We have been given access. When we pray, we are speaking directly to the King of Kings, and He delights in answering the prayers of His children.

So, why do we hesitate? Why do we doubt? Why do we hold back?

Sometimes, it's because we've been disappointed before. We prayed, and things didn't happen the way we expected. But sis, delayed does not mean denied. God's timing is perfect. His ways are higher. And just because you don't see the answer yet doesn't mean He isn't working on it.

Other times, we pray too safely because we don't fully grasp the power we have as women of faith. But I need you to shift your mindset today. Stop praying like your request is too big for God. Start praying like you already know He can do it. Speak His promises. Declare His Word. Believe for the impossible.

It's time to start praying like a woman who knows who she is in Christ. Pray like you believe mountains will move. Pray like chains are already breaking. Pray like healing is already happening. Because the truth is—it is. God is moving even now.

Your faith-filled prayers have the power to change your family, your finances, your health, your community, and even generations to come. So, don't hold back. Pray boldly. Pray with expectation. Pray knowing that God is able to do exceedingly, abundantly above all you could ask or think.

Because when a praying woman believes, nothing is impossible.

Declaration

Today, I declare that my prayers are powerful and bold. I will no longer pray timid prayers, but I will approach God with confidence, knowing that He is able to do more than I could ask or imagine. I declare that I will speak His promises over my life, my family, and my circumstances. I believe that mountains will move, chains will break, and healing is already happening. I will pray with faith, expecting God to do exceedingly, abundantly, above all I can think. I stand firm in the truth that nothing is impossible for me because I am a woman of faith in a BIG God. In Jesus' name, Amen.

Dr. Paulette Harper

WHEN WOMEN PRAY, HEAVEN MOVES

Prayer is not just something we do—it's who we are. It is the lifeline that connects us to the heart of God, the bridge between the natural and the supernatural, and the key to unlocking the promises of God in our lives. When a woman prays, something happens. And when women pray together, the enemy's plans crumble, chains break, and breakthroughs are released.

Throughout the Bible, we see the power of praying women. Hannah cried out in desperation, and God gave her Samuel. Esther fasted and prayed, and an entire nation was saved. The woman with the issue of blood reached out in faith, and her healing came instantly. These were women just like us—women who had burdens, struggles, and challenges but refused to let circumstances dictate their faith. They pressed in. They believed. And they saw God move.

Sisters, your prayers carry weight in the kingdom. Your words have power. When you pray, you're not just speaking into the air—you are shifting atmospheres, breaking generational curses, and calling forth things that are not as though they were. Your prayers matter.

Sometimes, the enemy tries to convince us that our prayers are ineffective. He whispers lies that say, "You've been praying for so long—nothing is changing." But I need you to hear this: Prayer is never wasted. Even when you don't see it, God is moving. Even when it feels like nothing is happening, heaven is working behind the scenes.

This is why we must be persistent in prayer. Pray when you feel strong. Pray when you feel weak. Pray when the answer seems close. Pray when the answer feels far away. And when you get weary, lean on your sisters. Let them remind you of who you are. Let them speak life into you. Let them stand in the gap when you don't have the words.

Because when women pray, heaven has no choice but to move.

Declaration

Today, I declare that my prayers are powerful and effective. I believe that when I pray, heaven moves. I declare that my words shift atmospheres, break chains, and bring forth breakthroughs. I choose to be persistent in prayer, knowing that God is always working behind the scenes. I stand firm in my faith, trusting that my prayers matter and are never wasted. I will lean on my sisters when I grow weary, knowing that together, we can accomplish great things in the kingdom. In Jesus' name, Amen.

Dr. Paulette Harper

CALLING ALL READERS!

Have you been uplifted and inspired by *Sisters Who Pray*? Your voice matters, and we would love to hear from you!

Share your thoughts, testimonies, and personal takeaways from the book by leaving a heartfelt review. Your words can help others discover the life-changing power of prayer and encourage more women to stand boldly in faith.

Here's how you can make a difference: Visit the book's page on your favorite online retailer. Leave an honest review sharing how *Sisters Who Pray* has impacted your faith and prayer life. Encourage your sisters, friends, and family to read the book and join this powerful movement of prayer.

Your reviews are a beacon of faith and encouragement, guiding others toward deeper intimacy with God through prayer.

Thank you for being part of this community of praying women and for spreading the message of faith, power, and breakthrough. Your support means everything!

Visionary Author Dr. Paulette Harper

www.pauletteharper.com

Thank you so much!!

OTHER BOOKS BY

DR. PAULETTE HARPER

Do you need a self-publishing coach?
Visit https://pauletteharper.com/services/

Solo Books

Fiction Inspirational

Secret <u>Places Revealed</u> (Award winner)
Living <u>Separate Lives</u>

Children

Princess Neveah: <u>Lessons of Self Discovery</u>

Nonfiction

That Was Then, This Is Now: <u>This Broken
Vessel Restored</u>
Completely <u>Whole</u>
Faith For <u>Every Mountain</u>

Coloring Book

The <u>Scriptures in Color</u>

Anthologies (Nonfiction)

The <u>Breaking Point</u>
When <u>Queens Rise</u>
For Such a <u>Time as This</u>
I Survived <u>The Storm</u>
Resilience in <u>Hard Times</u>
Women who <u>Soar</u>
Arise From <u>The Ashes</u>
Breaking <u>The Silence</u>
Her Unbreakable <u>Spirit</u>
Women with <u>Unshakable Faith</u>

Write A Book With Me

Do you have a story you want to share?

Would you like to be in our next anthology?

WHAT'S IN IT FOR YOU?

- Instant credibility for writing a best-selling book

- Your personal worth will increase

- Speaking opportunities will open for you

- Your personal finance will increase

- Your personal brand will be connected with other like-minded people

- Notoriety – Your circle of influence will increase and be empowered

JOIN ME!

I want to personally invite you to partner with me and join the waitlist for the next anthology offered by Visionary Author Dr. Paulette Harper

Visit https://pauletteharper.com/opportunities to get on the waitlist for the next book collaboration.

Author Coaching Services

Offered by Dr. Paulette Harper

Join us at One Story University Online School.

Unlock The Writer In You 90 Day Program

One Story University is an online school that provides aspiring authors with a step-by-step process on how to write and publish their self-help, how to, and personal story books in 90 days.

Visit <u>Unlock the Writer</u> to get access to the course.

A group coaching program for coaches, speakers, thought leaders, and entrepreneurs who are ready to write, self- publish and launch a best- selling book in 90 days.

5 Module Outline

Module 1- The Story Framework: The purpose behind your book, getting clarity on your story and creating the outline is the foundation every writer needs in order to produce a great book. The best writers are those who can frame the outline of their content, ensuring each chapter flows consistently and concisely for the reader.

Module 2- Crafting Your Story: Writers must know their ideal audience so they craft content that compels, sells, and propels their readers. Creating a premise and promise statement assures you will achieve all three.

Module 3- Constructing Your Book: Putting your book all together requires knowing what goes in the front and back of your book, as well as, hiring the right literary team to help put your book together.

Module 4- The Publishing Lab: Now you're ready to learn the steps to finally publishing your book and securing your intellectual property.

Module 5 – Promoting Your Book: Before you can promote yourself and your book, you must establish a customized and focused marketing plan. Bringing a new book to the market will require a strategy, a vision and proper planning in order to generate book sales.

www.ingramcontent.com/pod-product-compliance
Lightning Source LLC
Chambersburg PA
CBHW052008090426
42741CB00008B/1597